Walking with God in Truth, Healing and Deliverance

Wanakee M. Brown-Belin Prophetess

Chaplain FRC, IAC

BK Royston Publishing
P. O. Box 4321 | Jeffersonville, IN 47131
502-802-5385
http://www.bkroystonpublishing.com
bkroystonpublishing@gmail.com

© Copyright – 2020

All Rights Reserved. No part of this book may be reproduced, stored in a retrieval system, or transmitted by any means without the written permission of the author.

Cover Design: Gad – Elite Covers
Cover Image: BK Royston Photography
Illustrator on Page 82: Victor Keith Brown

ISBN-13: 978-1-951941-05-5

Scripture text used: King James Version
Public Domain
The Open Bible-Expanded Edition Copyright 1985
Thomas Nelson Inc
Biblehub.com 2004-2019

Printed in the United States of America

DEDICATION

This book is dedicated to my parents Clifford Lee Brown
Rebecca Beatrice Brown

My brothers Victor and Clifford
All of these people went so far beyond their duty to me, I can never repay them.

STATEMENT OF PASSION

I love to see acknowledgment of understanding a new concept.
I teach the word of God with passion and truth. It is my guide book.

www.womanofthewordministries.org

ACKNOWLEDGMENTS

It is sometimes very difficult to understand how any given situation can prepare you for future events. People are often put in positions to help other people without knowing they are doing so. This is true for me concerning this book. It is a compilation of events, crisis and traumas that I have been a part of. I have learned that information arises from pain, and the lessons are unforgettable. I acknowledge those who have crossed my path for the purposes of life's training.

Table of Contents

Dedication	iii
Statement of Passion	iv
Acknowledgements	v
Foreword	ix
Get Real	1
Seeking Truth	7
Roots	15
The Structure Walking with God Brings	27
The Fight is Real	41
Stability	67
Supernatural	83
About the Author	103

FOREWORD

One of the easiest things to do is to make excuses to give up. When you finally decide to give up, you think you feel a load lifted from your shoulders. Then I believe that there are levels of giving up. I've done this over my lifetime. The understanding that I have of my Father in heaven, who tells me that I'm never to give up on any level, has given me strength to thrive. I thank God for my increases daily. I'm open and honest with my Father. This openness gives me strength to take what is mine in Jesus name. I stand on His word, I'm glad to be a child of God.

GET REAL

Commitment, someone once said to me, "You think that you are in control of your life, you think you can make a real commitment, and you think you really have power." When you are young and full of delusions, the truth sounds so ridiculous. These statements were made to me by someone who I knew, but not someone I trusted. So, when someone I trusted made these same kinds of statements, and added, "You have a problem with commitment," I started to think about that. Now on the surface, anybody with eyes could see everything that surrounded me was full of commitment:

Grandparents married over 40 years

Parents married 52 years

Father and Mother worked the same job for 25 years

(There are more of these kinds of commitments in my life, but I think you can get an understanding of why I thought I had no problem at all with commitment.) The thing is, these commitments were made by other people and not me. Commitment does not rub off! I also learned, through experience, that not being able to commit can lead to a person simply being out of control. Now when you are out of control, then someone must come in and take control. This is where a problem could start, or a problem could be handled. There is no reason for you to feel like your life is out of control. Yet, so many Jesus lovers, God followers, and Christians feel like they have no control over their lives. I remember my mother asking God (remind me to tell you that story sometime) and accepting in faith that He would deliver. Why do some Christians find it hard to talk to God, the One who made them? Why do some people find it hard to take God at His word? The Word tells us that God loves us and only wants our success and happiness. We hear this but find it difficult to believe and "act on." We put faith in everyone and everything else in life and we are crushed, hurt, and dismayed beyond recognition and sometimes will hold on to the pain of a let-down by someone for years to come, creating a box or hole for ourselves and not being able to enjoy life to the fullest, in Matthew, it says we are caretakers of the earth. God is the only power that never changes, and He wants your success. I remember one of my school counselors saying to me that I would never amount to anything in life! I was just crazy enough to not believe her. On the other hand, I knew of someone who was told this same thing. This young lady wanted to go to medical school, not only did she not go to medical school, it took her quite a while to "gather" herself and make a life for herself and her five children. The negative information we accept on a regular basis sinks into our spirit and becomes a reality.

SEEKING TRUTH

Why not take and accept the reality of God's Word? Walking in God's Word is a lifestyle, and it must be cultivated. How, you might ask. There are nine fruits of the Spirit; gentleness and goodness are two of them. When you are reading the Bible, you must train yourself to think pleasant thoughts. God wants you to pray to Him and ask Him to remove every spirit that is not like Himself and to fill you with His spirit and holy things. God always remembers what we say, no matter what we say. We must stand strong and be willing to accept change in our lives. I know that any change is hard for no less reasons than we sometimes think we just figured it all out, and now we must start all over again. Also, sometimes people decide not to deal with you anymore if you turn out not to be a disappointment. We must develop a deep and meaningful relationship with God, and we cannot afford anything else or less. I am desperate for God and cannot live without Him. The more you seek Him, the more He will reveal Himself to you. It is when God reveals Himself to you that true joy will take place. There are mysteries of God, and there are things of God that, if you just open your eyes and your heart, you will see and hear from Him. God desires a loving relationship with us. I know sometimes we feel within ourselves that we are not good enough for God to love us and forgive us for our sins. We are sometimes embarrassed by our past sins, but the Word of God says we are forgiven, and God will remember our sins no more. We have a part to play as well. We must accept Jesus as our Lord and Savior, and we must know Him as both! God requires ALL. We cannot be selfish with our love; we must love God fully and be totally committed to Him! Our prayer life must be unstoppable, and we must grow our faith daily. There are some who would say that I am an expert at what I do. I take that same meaning and apply it to my relationship with Jesus. I want to be perfectly humble and transparent with my Lord, knowing that I am nothing without Him. He must lead me by the hand minute by minute! There should be no empty space or place within you. Empty spaces are dangerous; you should be filled daily, a fresh filling of the Holy Spirit. You should desire a clear mind, body, soul, and spirit. With a clear mind, you are better able to fight and withstand the enemy. As we engage in spiritual warfare and wear our full armor on a daily basis, 2 Corinthians 10:3-4 tells us that we walk in the flesh, but we do not fight or war in the flesh. If this was the case, we would lose every battle, because the flesh is weak! Jesus said that we have complete power over the devil and that we are to fight every day. We are not only to fight for ourselves but for others. Intercessory prayer and warfare are trusting God to bring change and deliverance to someone who is in need. One of the most powerful weapons that we have at our disposal is LOVE. This is the single most overlooked weapon that the child of God has! Love is one of the nine fruits of the Spirit, and it can bring the enemy to his knees! You can love someone past their pain and bring them into God's wonderful presence. To me, love is a quiet, gentle weapon that should not be overlooked. We are not alone. According to Acts 1:5, we have the promise of the Holy Ghost, who is our comforter, and the Holy Spirit fills us with supernatural power. We have nothing to fear. We simply take God at His word and move forward in love and truth. Our passion for God must outweigh everything else, and we must run to Him with open arms.

ROOTS

You can learn a lot from watching people. My mother was a quiet, refined woman who knew how to pray. It is the single most important thing you can do for others. Prayer to God pleases Him, and it really shows how much you love others to trust them to God with your prayers. When you live the word of God, it does not matter who you are; for example, mother, wife, employer, teacher, student or employee. You move through each "person" with ease and confidence knowing that God is an all-powerful and never-changing God, knowing that all of your needs are met, and you have nothing to fear. The Bible is the one and the only source from which instruction can be taken concerning the knowledge of God and the duties required of us by our Creator. It is our daily guide on how to live every aspect of our lives. We must pray, in truth, to keep our spirits and minds strong. We must care for our physical bodies because we are the caretakers. It is our duty, to the best of our ability, to return our bodies back to our Creator in the same condition it was given to us. We are spirits, and our bodies are our earthly homes. Eating a healthy diet and being physically active should be a part of our daily routine. When you realize who you are in Christ (His child), you can own every situation and conquer it, no questions asked! God wants you happy and close to Him. He wants an intimate relationship with you. God's love is pure and tender. We are to be totally committed to Him and pray a prayer of commitment. We cannot do that apart from God's grace. Women tend to fall into commitments very easy; it is in a woman's nature to do so, most often without question. Sometimes, even if the relationship is not good and loving, we stay in it for fear of being alone, fear of change, and fear of failure (even though being in a failed relationship is counterproductive). We will not have to justify or rationalize our relationship with God. Once we make the commitment to the Father and fully embrace Him, the love is unmatched. God does not care what you look like. We are all made in His image. God wants us in a loving human relationship, as He made man and women for one another. God is always first in our lives. Women, we are not to be victims of love! We should be growing daily in the knowledge of our Father and in understanding who we are and how to treat others that we might find ourselves in relationships with. We all have a starting point.

GIFTS OF THE SPIRIT

There are nine gifts of the Spirit, and they are supernatural.
I Corinthians 12:7-11
These gifts are:

1. The word of wisdom
2. The word of knowledge
3. Faith
4. Gifts of healing
5. Working of miracles
6. Prophesy
7. Discerning of tongues
8. Kinds of tongues
9. Interpretation of tongues

There are nine fruits of the spirit.
Galatians 5:22-23
These fruits are:

1. Love
2. Joy
3. Peace
4. Longsuffering
5. Gentleness
6. Goodness
7. Faith
8. Meekness
9. Temperance

We are to practice the fruits and gifts of the spirit. Often times, we don't want to show outward affection for God, most want to keep God in a box and love Him on our terms. What if God loved us on His terms? What if God treated us like we treat Him? I know that this question has been over asked, but have you really stopped to think about the answer! God does not want waxed-over love. My Bible tells me in Revelations 3:16 that God will spit you out of His mouth for being lukewarm. He wants true praise. There is never any emotional pain associated with loving God. He sends His Son and the Holy Spirit to us so we would be completely covered. Sometimes people (from my experiences it's mostly women) feel like they must earn the right to enjoy life, and most people don't feel that they have earned the right, guilt sets in with the very thought that we serve a God who wants us happy on a daily basis! God gives us what we cannot earn, and that is salvation. He gives it freely; you trust Him knowing that you can never be good enough, but that He loves you! It's the total trust and faith in Him. This is God, and He gets all of the credit. If we could buy or work hard enough for His goodness, we would think we are the ones who deserve the pat on the back. God does have rules which are for your own good. There is much structure in service to God. Spiritual meditation is the kind of medication I like, and we must take it in massive doses daily! When you are strong in spirit, you are better prepared to go into battle. A lot of us are simply unprepared. Daily prayer is a major weapon in the battle. Your relationship with your Owner and Maker keeps you strong. Our God is a Holy and all-consuming fire. I hunger for God, and my heart aches to be closer to Him. Do you think God owes you something, or do you think you owe something to God? We know God so loved the world John 3:16 that He gave His only Son, notwithstanding you still have a choice. You can choose to develop a mighty relationship with Him, or not! It's up to you. Our Lord and Savior is goodness and light, and the opposite of that is darkness and shame. I choose to bring heaven down to earth on a daily basis. It took some time for the full understanding of that statement to manifest in my life. As the word of God is food to me and His spirit is life for me, I look at the world as open to me to achieving anything under the sun in the mighty name of Jesus. It will take work on your part; no reasonable person can expect to achieve without planning and working a plan.

THE STRUCTURE WALKING WITH GOD BRINGS

Simply moving from place to place without a true plan is just wasteful. We all have basic needs that must be met. Thank God for this, but do not beg Him to do what He has given you the ability to do. It wastes time, and He does not like that. I have, over the years, asked for forgiveness for wasting precious time. I spent time trying to fit in where God did not want me to. I chose all the easy fixes, and the results were distractions. As a woman, I had and have a need to belong; this is normal and good.

Women have the need for quick, trustworthy information. We need answers to our questions to make us feel secure. The need to belong is very strong in women, and the need to belong will drive some women to do some incredible things. Unfortunately, some of these things can impair our judgment and not allow us to think clearly. There is an old joke, or story, about a nearsighted woman who has lost her keys late at night and is looking for them by the light of a streetlamp. Another person comes along and offers to help her, and asks, "Are you sure this is where you lost them?" The lady answers, "No, but this is where the light is." So many of us search for what is missing in our lives not where it can be found, but where it is easy to look! It is true that you will need to look below the surface for the truth. We know the Word of God says, "Seek, and you will find." We are to actively seek the Lord. There is a place in you that only Jesus can fill. Develop a loving and intimate relationship with God. Speak to Him with your whole heart and worship Him in love. Your prayers are a reflection of your love for your Owner and Maker. Prayer can be as simple as talking to God. A growing child of God will also grow in their prayer life! Make a commitment to pray to your Father on a daily basis. You will find it easier and easier to do. Be the role model and show your family and friends just how enjoyable it is to be in loving contact with God. The change in you is what people will see. We also have a duty to pray for others. Prayers should not be selfish in nature. It is perfectly fine to ask God for what you want, but you must think of others when you pray. This includes praying for our enemies Matthew 5:43-44. When you can truly pray for someone else, including your enemies, you are spiritually growing in Jesus

Christ and growth is necessary for a child of God. Remember always to lean on the Holy Spirit, as He is your helper. From situation to situation, He will be there to guide you. You should always be fully protected by having on your entire armor of God, and you use it to:

Pray for those who despitefully use you.

Pray for those who lie on you.

Pray for those who try to ruin your name.

Galatians 2:20 says, "I am crucified with Christ; nevertheless I live, yet not I but Christ liveth in me and the life which I now live in the flesh, I live by the faith of the Son of God, who loved me and gave Himself for me." God also said lean not unto your own understanding. We are to remain humble and open to His leading. The Bible is your guidebook for your life. We must carry our cross daily and seek the Lord with all our hearts. Everything that is connected to God is about love, make no mistake about that. The Bible is very clear as to what you will receive by following the Word in every respect, and blessings will flow to you, so much so that you will feel overwhelmed. All blessings come from God on the basis of faith, not law. The law declares men guilty and keeps them bound. Faith sets men free to enjoy liberty in Christ. Freedom in Christ means freedom to produce the fruits of righteousness through a spirit-led lifestyle. Women often feel the need to measure their success in life by the things they have accomplished, but how do you really measure success? I believe it is measured by your constant growth in Christ! Everyone has a starting point, and there is no need to feel bad about that. When you are young, you grow physically, and a child of God should never stop growing spiritually. I believe the best indicator of growth is your understanding of the need to give. When we give, it makes us richer on a spiritual level. 1 Corinthians 16:2 has principles, if you will, concerning giving.

1. My giving is to be regular (on the first day of the week [tithes]).
2. My giving is to be systemic (set aside what you are giving); this does not include tithes.
3. My giving is to be proportionate (as God has prospered you, this does not include tithes).

Warning: Failure to honor God with money is a very serious matter. God does not need money. When you give you exhibit faith in His word and the money goes to further the kingdom work. I know there are problems within churches concerning money, and much prayer is consuming believers who are praying and expecting a "cleaning" within churches. Don't make the mistake of thinking you can hold on to your money until people in churches come to their senses! The blessings are in giving it in faith with a cheerful heart. God promises abundant blessings for those who honor Him with money, and God does not lie. All these money principles are found within the word of God. I look at the Bible as my "holy google book." I find answers there for every question that I ask. God serves us in pure love, and we are to serve one another in the same way. Love is very powerful and is almost always overlooked. I am convinced that if we knew how much God loves us, we would truly live differently. This has to do with wanting God on our terms. We want to keep God in a safe spot and have Him come into our lives at the very moment we want Him. We never want to go through or carry our cross for Him.

We never want to stand up for Him, and mostly we are ashamed of Him before people. So, when we are at our lowest, and we feel we are not worthy of love from Him or anyone, we fail to understand the depth of His love for us. If we understood the Father-child relationship, we would know that parents' discipline is not always fun for the child. Children should obey their parents, even if it is not something that they want to do! Total commitment and honor are what God requires; in other words, God requires ALL! A set lifestyle and a set mindset are a requirement for the child of God. You think on what is good in your life. I know this is not easy. You must make a strong effort, it will become a habit, and most often when you shift your mindset you will find that people will think less of you. So, you are moving into a more positive place and becoming stronger, and as this happens you are becoming less popular with your crowd. Thus, you find you are outgrowing the "what was" bunch. Positive "+" and negative "-" The positive symbol even looks stronger. The circumstances that arise in your life simply provide you with the opportunity to show-off-your-faith in Jesus. A lot of us operate under the assumption that daily life is a one-man-one-woman battleground. While daily life is a battleground, we are not alone in our fight.

THE FIGHT IS REAL

Our loving Daddy fights with and for us. I think, mostly, that women cannot think clearly if they are surrounded by confusion, clutter, and chaos. I call this the "deadly three C's." This often leads to self-torture; it's a bad habit, and it only makes the enemy happy. We as children of God must connect to our Father in the most effective way, and that is through prayer. It's pure talk with God, and it should also always be honest talk. God knows anyway, but He wants us to admit everything to Him; what makes us happy and what makes us sad. This creates intimacy with God as well. We all need intimacy with God as our Father. The loving and intimate relationship God had and has with His Son, Jesus, our Lord and Savior, is pure love. Going deeper into what prayer can do for us, I mean that praying is an act of faith. Jesus is our example for all things in life, and if Jesus did nothing while He was walking the earth, He prayed! He prayed for strength to overcome at times of weakness. He prayed for faith at times to bring the unbelieving into faith. He prayed for His fellowman! Prayer is not difficult or hard. We sometimes think we are not worthy of any good gift from above, and because of our disobedience our prayers will not even be heard. While it is true our prayers can be hindered (and that is not God's fault), we should move in faith and line our lives up with the word as we pray. We communicate minute by minute with our family, friends, co-workers, church members, and people on the street. It only makes good sense to communicate with the One who made us. Jesus is our example, and just as He prayed and gave praise to the Father, we are to do the same. Prayer is a relationship and one that we truly need. We are to depend upon

Jesus like our life depended on it because it does. We speak to our Maker in a loving way, we ask for guidance in everything that we are doing, and we take every need and give it to God. The yoke of Jesus is light, and He gives it to us Matthew 11:28-30. If drama and chaos have always been present in your life; you might find it hard to gauge your own feelings, embracing pain and disappointment as normal. It is not, and we are designed to love and have love shown to us. God loves you, and this is your base. If no one else does, He does! This love will encourage you to do whatever is needed to move forward in a mighty way. Sometimes it seems that forward movement and any changes in your life seem to make things worse. You know you are loved, you are walking in faith, and you must SHIFT. You maintain your balance and your positive (+), through your relationship with Jesus. Jesus said that today's trouble is enough. Put no thought into worrying about tomorrow for tomorrow will take care of itself. Your response to your suffering determines the result. All of your actions must be above reproach. You must police yourself daily. I know this is much easier said than done because you must be honest with yourself. It's hard to look yourself in the mirror and admit you have said something that you should not have said or done something you know to be wrong. Most people who believe in Jesus and what He stood for, make excuses and tell themselves there is no need to speak about what was done because God already knows everything. There is something about a personal relationship with God that requires us to speak aloud the things that happen in our lives. God wants to hear you say it, and then come to Him and talk to Him about it. This builds trust with your Maker. This also tells the enemy you have nothing to hide, as the enemy always wants to bring up your "deleted" past. I use the word "deleted" because this is what God does with it if you ask Him to. Tackling everything in your life is hard, but it keeps you on your toes. When you take care of your own life, you don't have time to dibble and dabble in someone else's life. The objective is to live above the circumstances. We have the great example of Jesus who did that before us. So, we read our Word, learn what He did, and follow His footsteps. So let me repeat, we must read our Bible, it is our guide book, it's not a Book so you can pick out verses to "brow-beat" your fellow man with it. In other words, we don't go to the Bible when we see someone doing wrong, find a verse and say, "Read this, you are making a mistake." When we do Kingdom work, we tell people who God is and how He has helped you in your life. We offer help to others to understand that God loves them too. We do not judge anyone because we truly do not know what another person is going through. What you say to a person could change their very existence. We also seek elders (an elder is someone who knows more than you do). We ask for advice and guidance. This should be done in your local church as we all must be covered under the five-fold ministry. I know some of us don't think it's necessary to be a member of a local church because there are so many things that are going wrong within the church. This is all the more reason why we need to be there to make sure we are treating the church and God's people properly. It is the Bride of Christ, and He is coming back for her. There will be trouble, but we have the formula to rise above the trouble. Although this is a truth of God, most believers simply do not live this truth. The church is supposed to represent freedom from the world for the children of God. We are to bring heaven down to earth, on a daily basis, showing the enemy and his workers who is the boss! Believers are pledged with guilt, and this seems to paralyze the mind as to the power we have through Jesus Christ. There is nothing you can do to earn the blessings of God. He gives salvation freely so you will totally depend on Him. If you could earn it, it would not be a gift. God will take care of you, from the top of your head to the soles of your feet! You must live by the Word and be open and honest with Him.

We are to adopt a Christ-like attitude and minister to others and expect nothing in return. WARNING: You must go where God directs you to go and do what God directs you to do and not do what you want to do. You will know what you are to do when you develop a personal relationship with Him, so listen for His voice and follow it. The Lord Jesus is the source of full knowledge and power for the attainment of spiritual maturity, 2 Peter 2:7-8 states, that you must guard your eye and ear gates so you will not be subject to ungodliness and evil. Even a righteous man cannot maintain in the midst of evil, day in and day out. You must never operate out of your emotions or feelings. The Lord Jesus is our guide. We are supposed to look at His life on earth and understand what He had to go through and see His reaction and His attitude and handle any situation the way He did and would have. He is our example. I'll tell you something else, we are to make disciples of others. Jesus did that with His disciples and others. God is your Father, Jesus is the door, The Holy Spirit is your guide, and prayer is the catalyst! As you grow your relationship with God, you will become more aware of Him. We were designed to have a very personal relationship with Him. He will reveal to you things you need to know and things you would like to know. You might ask yourself how would I ever know? When we read our Bible (we should be reading our Bible's daily), we are to ask for understanding of God's Word, He will bring the understanding in many different ways. In 1 John 2:5 it says (paraphrased), "But whoever keeps His word (the Bible) in Him is the love of God perfected, then we know we are in Him." I now want to go a bit deeper into the roles that women play in their families.

Women have a tremendous power to influence. WARNING: The woman is the helpmate of the man. The man, biblically, is the head of the household. Serving God, totally without question, is the starting point. When the household has this truth, all things after this will fall into place. Without a doubt it will be difficult, but there is growth in difficulty and in pain. God could not teach us if He could not inflict some pain into our lives. I can say without a doubt, the pain I had to experience in my life taught me how to communicate successfully with God. I found personal healing through being totally transparent with God! In finding myself, I am better able to help another person. There are so many secrets women keep. We are very good at living in a made-up life. We sometimes think if we say something, it's true! We tell others our dreams, what we want to happen, but make no actual move to achieve them. Most of us don't even know how to start to prepare for a dream. The enemy will come to you and keep you in a sort of fog. You speak something, and a form of pride kicks in telling you that you don't need to do anything else. After all, you have voiced it and put it in the universe, now all you have to do is sit back and watch your dream take place. WRONG! Preparation for how we live day by day takes so much work on our part. Everything we are and all that we do is spiritual first. So, it makes good sense to praise our Owner and ask for instructions before we do anything. We can tell God our hopes and dreams and ask what He thinks. WARNING: It is in your best interest to wait for the answers from God as to what you are to do. Yes, God knows all, but it builds a personal and intimate relationship with Him when you trust Him enough to ask His opinion. When we don't and go off in several different directions, we fall on our faces, end up hurting, end up broken-hearted, and feeling very alone, then the first person we blame is God. We say something like this, "How could God let something like this happen to me? I'm a good person, now look at the mess I'm in." I know without a shadow of a doubt that if we ask for help, we will receive help. Let me tell you this, and I believe that I've said this before, God requires ALL, and that's all of your time, affection, love, mind, body, and soul! When you become a slave to God you are totally free. You will reach your full potential in this life, and you will lift others up to Christ. It is not about you; it's about working for the kingdom of God. The things you want in life will come your way as you are obedient to God. The concept of being a slave to Jesus is consistent in every area of life. Since you were bought and paid for by the precious blood of Jesus. Ask yourself these questions:

1. Why am I not feeling genuine joy? (In any given situation)
2. Am I willing to really let God use me?

Really think about question number 2. People jump right in on this one, "Oh yes. God can use me." They do not fully understand this concept. It is most joyful when we fully surrender to Him and allow Him to work through us. The Bible tells us to be careful about how you entertain strangers because there have been some that have entertained angels not being aware they have done so. You must live your life in a fashion that will make people want to know more about the God you serve. I also want to tell you that there is only one way to God and it's through His son Jesus Christ. So, when you know this, you know that you are serving the one true God because God and Jesus cannot be separated. The

Holy Spirit is the third part of the two. No other religion or no one who you could possibly believe in can boast of a resurrection of their god. Only Jesus was sent by the Father to die on a cross, sit in hell to overcome the enemy, then rise on the third day having defeated the enemy and having all power in His hand. This was done for us so our lives can reflect the beautiful sacrifice that Jesus made for us. We are "gods" before God. He gave us the earth to caretake. We cannot step before God and do what we want to do. When humans think they know more than God, all hell literally breaks loose. The enemy enters and fowls up the thought process. Think about it, before the devil was cast out of heaven, he thought he was better than God. Why would you think the devil would not be telling you that you can just do whatever you want like he did. He did and got booted out of heaven. Speaking of the enemy, I want to talk about one of his tricks, which is shame. He will use shame to keep you from even thinking that God loves you. I feel that shame is dealt with differently by women than men. I must speak from a woman's standpoint because I am a woman. I think that shame, guilt, and self-hatred are kind of all rolled into one. Before we can deal with our shame before God, we start to feel guilty, and we continue with the guilt and start beating up on ourselves, which leads to self-hate. When we deal with self-hate, we become isolated and lonely. For all of us, when we become lonely, degrees of desperation set in. Now our families and loved ones are affected. Sound judgment can sometimes take a back seat, and we reach for anything and anyone to help reduce the pain we are feeling. I want to tell you there is a place in you that only God can fill. I know some of you have felt so empty at times that you felt like you could not go on. This is what the enemy wants you to do, quit, give up, become despondent, and hopeless. There is something else that we do, which I refer to as "self-torture." We compare ourselves to other people. God made each and every one of us unique, and He knows all about us. He does not compare us to one another. We all have varying gifts that the Holy Spirit gave us to use. It's the enemy telling you that no matter how hard you work, you will never be able to measure up to another person when, in reality, you are not supposed to measure up to anyone else. You are special in your own right; your gifts are yours to glorify God. I can recall a time in my life when I was "off-center." I needed focus, and I needed a push. My Heavenly Father, my Savior, my Owner, and Maker said to me one day, "Read your Bible." I heard these words as plain as someone standing next to me would speak. Also, at this time in my life evil spirits were following me around. I knew this and, every now and then, I could rebuke them. I knew they were pesky, but I also knew without a doubt that God was protecting me and my angels were around me. I actually witnessed a discussion between the enemy and God concerning my life. I'll speak more about this at the end of the book.

STABILITY

Now, studying the Word daily is very important. You noticed I said study, not just read! You receive strength from the Word that can only be obtained this way. It is living water for your soul. Sometimes when we read the Word, we become confused and offended. We don't want to change the way we live or the things we do. We want God only on our terms. Like any good Father, He will tell you what you are doing wrong or right. We don't want to hear anything about what we might be doing wrong. You can ask God questions if you want to. You can tell Him what you are feeling, and you can even tell Him that you are upset with Him. Believe it or not, this type of situation helps build your relationship with God. The experiences in your life help to mold and shape you into the person God wants you to be. He sets you up so He can use you. These experiences include hurt, pain, betrayal, bitterness, and every other emotion you can think of. God will allow any and everything to happen because He does not condone sin. Ask yourself a serious question: Are you someone who can win people to

Christ? This is the posture we are to hold every minute of our lives. We will make mistakes. When we do, we are to go to God and tell Him of our mistakes and ask Him to forgive us, be convicted by the Holy Spirit, and let the blood of Jesus wash us clean. We never have to believe the lies of the enemy, who will tell us stuff like:

God will not forgive you.

God will always remember what you do wrong.

God will hold what you do wrong against you for the rest of your life.

Remember when I asked you if you could win someone to Christ? When you find your answer, this could be a starting point for you. Come as you are! Commit yourself fully to God. You are a complete package uniquely made by God, just as you are. God did not make a mistake when He made you. To be a person God can use requires you to embrace yourself in love fully. To embrace yourself, you must love yourself. I know this sounds easy, but it can sometimes be very hard to do for some of us. You must know the condition of your heart.

Searching yourself can be painful because, as you search, you uncover fears, insecurities, and judgments. We are not to judge ourselves or others. We must come before God broken and empty. We can change the world by letting God use us. Pray this prayer of emptying so you can be used by God to do His work:

Dear Father, I love you, and I know that you loved me in the womb. I come before you empty, and I am willing to be filled by you daily to be enabled to go and do the work you require me to do. Nothing is more important to me than that. In Jesus mighty name, Amen.

Look what God has promised you. Psalms 1:1-3 says, "Blessed is the man who does not walk in the counsel of the wicked or stand in the way of sinners or sit in the seat of mockers. But his delight is in the law of the Lord, and on His law, he meditates day and night. He is like a tree planted by streams of water which yields its fruit in season and whose leaf does not wither, and whatever he does shall prosper." What a loving God we serve! Abide in His Word, and His Word will abide in you. Wear your full armor daily to be fully prepared to do battle. Peter, an apostle of Jesus Christ, urges you as a lover of Jesus to keep a close watch on your personal life. Jesus' way of life demands personal sacrifice in pursuing knowledge, virtue, patience, godliness, and love. We are reminded that although God may be long-suffering in sending judgment, nevertheless, it will come. It is far better to obey, and there are rewards in obedience! There is a relationship between God and His people. I can say, without a doubt, that it is very unequal. God puts up with our selfish attitudes, our jealousy, and our childish behavior. He cares for us far more than we deserve. God does not want us in pain. Yes, we will experience pain in the things God will teach us. Have you ever heard the expression, there is knowledge in pain. For some of us the experience of pain is the only way we can learn. Now back to God does not want us in pain. God is love, and there is no pain associated with loving Him. I am convinced that if we knew how much God loves us, it would change every aspect of our lives. We love God faithfully. In that faith, we must endure trials and tests, which we should face head-on! We already have the victory. When you exercise your faith, you will be tempted, but faithfulness will keep you on track. Faith stands up when all else fails. Faith will let you choose to separate from worldly things and grow closer to your Owner and Maker. One thing I love about God is that He has thought of absolutely everything! We have all the help we need in the Holy Spirit. He is our Helper. He will take care to show us spiritual things. He will help us to remember past events that have haunted us for years, and He will bring healing to our minds. Our private prayer time with God is very important, and it is our connection point to Him. It is beyond important to pray daily. I think that we should be "emptied" daily and be filled again with the presence of God! There is nothing more powerful than a person being at peace with themselves and others, knowing that God has your back! But always count it all joy when you face tests, as tests develop perseverance. You may ask yourself, "What does it take to be a person of God?" I'll tell you first what it does not take, and that is for you to be perfect. God does not require a perfect vessel; He requires a clean one. It takes a clean vessel so God can use you to fulfill His purpose on this earth. Jesus is our example. He was called names, He was accused of being in cahoots with the Devil, and His own brothers did not even believe in Him (I'm not for sure even if they liked Him). So, if Jesus had to endure these hardships, what do you think we as ones who proclaim His goodness and His name will have to put up with. He carried His cross, and we must pick it up daily and carry it. We are to just deliver the message; once done, we have done our job. People may not like it or like you, but it is what we must do as we are obeying God. People might dismiss you, but God never will. Pray in faith for the things of God to be manifested in the earth realm as it is in heaven, and it will be so! Do not expect people to cheer you on, did they cheer Jesus on? We are His disciples. What He went through, we will have to go through! We all deserve more than the worse thing we can stand (or take). Your success is guaranteed in the mighty name of Jesus. I ask you, in all sincerity, to pray daily and develop a true and honest relationship with God. In my opinion, you need to pray like you need to breathe. You want to stay in step with God <u>so you can be</u>

<u>where He is and not where He was!</u> There is so much power in prayer. You can always depend on God in the most personal and intimate way. Sometimes we feel embarrassed by any shortcomings that we see in our lives. No one is perfect, and we all have shortcomings. We all need to work on ourselves. If you ask, God will forgive your sins no matter what the sin is. We must seek God like our lives depend on it (because it does). Let me ask a few questions. Do you believe that God sent His son Jesus to save you? If your answer is yes, do you truly accept Jesus Christ as your Savior? If your

answer is yes, you have taken the first step to a lifelong loving relationship that will never fail you! There is nothing more powerful than people who accept and know Jesus as their Lord and Savior. Children of the King!

PLANT AND BARE GOOD FRUIT
Plant 5 rows of peas:
Prayer
Perseverance
Politeness
Promptness
Purity

PLANT 3 ROWS OF SQUASH

Squash gossip

Squash criticism

Squash indifference

PLANT 5 ROWS OF LETTUCE

Let us be faithful to duty

Let us not be selfish

Let us truthful

Let us love one another

Let us follow Christ

NO GARDEN IS COMPLETE WITHOUT TURNUPS

Turn up for church

Turn up with a smile

Turn up with new ideas

Turn up with determination to make everything count for something good and worthwhile
-Unknown source-

SUPERNATURAL

I call this last chapter of my book, Supernatural. I am simply writing about the things that happened to me over the years of my life. These testimonies still give me hope of a God who loves all of us beyond anything that we deserve. I tell these testimonies from time to time to inspire others. My hope is that when you read my words, your faith will increase as every word you will read is the truth. When I was going through these experiences, I would ask God what He wanted me to do with them. I prayed for a sound mind and that I would keep my right mind, as these experiences are truly supernatural. May you be strengthened and blessed by the reading.

WHY GOD STILL LET ME HAVE TEN WHOLE FINGERS

I don't remember exactly how old I was, but I was a kid. Like any kid, I wanted to be involved in what was going on in my house, especially the kitchen, being a girl and all. Dinner was being prepared, and I wanted to help. I picked up a knife to cut some of the vegetables, it was a big knife, and my Mom did not see me pick it up. I posed to cut the carrot and brought the large knife right down on the forefinger of my left hand. I screamed, and my mom rushed me to the sink to run water under my hand, then my hand was wrapped up, and we went to the Emergency Room. When I finally saw my finger, I saw my finger cut clear up to the first bone because I actually saw the bone sticking out. The doctor wrapped up my finger and did not say a word. He left the room with my mom, they reentered the room, and we went home. I never saw the old tip of my finger, but within months my finger had grown back. To this day I have a rough spot where my finger grew back.

Scripture reference:
Jeremiah 30:17
Isaiah 53:4-5

PEOPLE JUST WANT TO TELL ME

I was a teenager still living at home with my father, mother, and two brothers. It was a Saturday. Back when I was growing up, all the kids would get up, make beds and get ready for breakfast. One of my friend's older sister came to me and said, "I saw a devil in the corner of my room." I said, "What did you do?" She said, "I just made my bed up and got out of there." I said, "What are you going to do about it?" I saw what the devil looked like sitting in the corner of her room. Over my life, I had someone else tell me about a devil sitting in the corner of a room.

Scripture reference:

Proverbs 25:12

James 1:19

I CAN SEE THAT

I was sitting and talking to a guy, and I was in my 20's. It was just a normal conversation about a little bit of everything. All of a sudden, I saw what he really looked like. I did a double-take and turned up my nose. He looked at me kind of puzzled like. He did not ask me what was wrong. His true face was very distorted, his eyes were uneven, and his face was on fire.

Scripture reference:

John 3:3

Ephesians 1:15-19

GOD SAID NO

This happened in the year 2006. It did not happen on June 6, but in this year when God revealed this to me, it had been going on for a while. I could tell the difference between God and the Devil. The best way I can describe Him, and the Devil is to say that God was calm, and the Devil was angry. The Devil told God that he wanted to kill me. God said, "This is my child. You cannot do that, but I will allow you to bother her." I saw God as a Spirit and the Devil as a man.

Scripture reference:

Genesis 3:1-4

Ezekiel 28:12-13

WATCH YOUR MOUTH

I was a kid. My friends and I thought one day that it would be a good idea to use every cuss word that we could think of. So, we went to the playground and started to cuss until the sun went down. Later we went to our own homes. I got ready for bed, said my prayers, and hopped into bed. Closer toward morning, I pulled the covers down from my body to turn over in the bed. I looked up and I saw the prettiest angel standing by my bed.

I do not know how long she had been standing there, but when I looked at her, she smiled and turned and walked through the closet door. I said, "Ok, I'm done cussing."

Scripture reference:
Luke 6:45
James 3:10

SO KIND

Again, while I was in bed, there was an angel standing near the wall facing me from the bottom of the bed. She said, "It's time for you to get up." I woke up, but it did not feel as if I was asleep. I felt wisdom, love, and kindness of this angel. It was so much wisdom, it overwhelmed me.

Scripture reference:
Revelation 4:8
2 Samuel 14:17

YES, I HEARD YOU

I was in my 30's and I wanted to hang out with some particular people. Now, when I first decided to do this, I looked at them and it was so much darkness and lies, as I was looking, I saw blackness and turmoil. People were screaming and confused. I was still on my way to be with these people. The Holy Spirit said in a calm voice, "Don't do this." I heard it as someone speaking. I was still preparing to go, and The Holy Spirit said again, "Don't do this." I heard it as someone speaking. I was still preparing to go, and the Holy Spirit screamed at me and said, "Don't do this!" I'm thankful the Holy Spirit did not give up on me telling me three times not to do something that clearly was not in my best interest.

Scripture reference:

Ezekiel 2:2

John 16:13

THIS HOUSE IS WHAT?

I knew exactly what I was doing when I went to this guy's house to hang out. When I got there, I found the house full of people. I later learned that some of the people lived there, and some of the people were there because they did not have anywhere else to go. Others were just there to people watch. Needless to say, the house was full of all kinds of people. When I walked in, a woman came up to me and looked me directly in my face and said, "You know this house is haunted." Now I was there (in my opinion) to do something I really did not feel good about doing, so I quickly responded, "So. I serve God." She said, "Okay." In the wee hours of the night, as I lay in the bed next to this guy, I was picked up and tossed around. Now I was still sleeping and did not fully comprehend what was happening to me. Then I was aware of something that was directly in my face. Now I woke up, and I just brushed my hand in front of my face. I was picked up again and tossed around in the bed. Now I was just annoyed and trying to get some sleep. I opened my mouth and said, "Father, will you tell him to leave me alone?" I saw the evil spirit flee with a frightening look on his face. I went back to sleep until morning, got up, and went home.

Scripture reference:
Luke 4:8
Ephesians 6:11

THE DEVIL TRIED TO SHUT MY MOUTH

Everywhere in the world there are places that the enemy is invited into. Invited by people. Sometimes unknowingly and sometimes by the people who serve him. I went to a place where he was invited. I did not know it at first, but when I got there I knew. I should have immediately turned and walked out. I did not. A part of me was curious as to how his kids reacted. This was a strip mall. As I was walking through, I did see some nice items. I also stopped and spoke to some people. Spiritually these people knew who I was and I knew who they were. I kept shopping. I purchased some videos, a tee top and a bracelet. I went to my car and got in and said a prayer over what I purchased. I knew that God was with me but I also knew that I should have walked out as soon as I entered the store. I looked at the videos I purchased and three them on the ground. I kept the bracelet and the top. I went on with my day and got into the bed about 10:00 p.m. Sometime between 2 a.m. and 3 a.m. I felt like my mouth was glued shut. I was speaking muffled trying to open my mouth and speak. I kept pushing in the Spirit to free myself. I felt as if my arms and my chest were being held down. I kept pushing in the spirit. I broke free and immediately started to praise God. I started praying in the spirit. I took the bracelet and the tee shirt to the big garbage can outside of my house at between 2 a.m. and 3 a.m. I took one item at a time, so that I made 2 trips all of the while praying in the spirit. I came back into my home, went back to bed and slept like a baby in the arms of the Lord. This is the 2nd time that this kind of thing has happened to me. I thank God for His protection over me. I thank Him that He has given me the power in His name to completely destroy the enemy!

Scripture reference is:
Psalms 46: 1-3
Matthew 4:10
1 John 5:4

About the Author

I was called to the Ministry at the age of 10 years. As The Holy Spirit was guiding me, telling me that the journey would be difficult but rewarding. This book is 10 years in the making. It is not the size of the book but the insight it holds. In this day and time when everyone is an expert at everything, a simple guide to "walking" is much needed. There are times when a "thing" can be known but simply overlooked due to saturation. This book is a guide and a reminder of how to unravel the complexities of a simple concept.
Blessings.

Wanakee Marie Brown-Belin

- Licensed and Ordained Minister
- Prophetess
- Ordained Chaplain
- Founder of Woman of the Word Ministry/HEARTMAKEOVERS Program
- Founder of the ALPHAWOMAN1 Program
- Founder of Healthyskin by Seasons
- Co-Author of The Smell of Poverty
- Speaker

http://www.womanofthewordministries.org/

www.ingramcontent.com/pod-product-compliance
Lightning Source LLC
Chambersburg PA
CBHW071222160426
43196CB00012B/2381